ENDGAME

POETRY *of* RETIREMENT

OTHER RECENT BOOKS *by* GRADY MEANS

The New Enlightenment, A Search for Global Civilization,
Peace, and Spiritual Growth in the 21st Century
(Two Harbors, 2010)

MetaCapitalism: The E-Business Revolution and the Design
of 21st Century Companies and Markets
(Wiley, 2000)

Wisdom of the CEO
(Wiley, 2000)

E-Government 2001
(Rowman and Littlefield, 2001)

ENDGAME

POETRY *of* RETIREMENT

GRADY MEANS

MILL CITY PRESS

Mill City Press, Inc.
212 3rd Avenue North, Suite 290
Minneapolis, MN 55401
612.455.2294
www.millcitypublishing.com

ISBN-13: 978-1-938223-80-8
LCCN: 2012918359

Cover Design and Typeset by Madge Duffy

Printed in the United States of America

CONTENTS

❧

AUTHOR'S INTRODUCTION   ix

THE SPIRIT   1
Fixed Income   3
"Sir"   7
Fogged In   11
Witnesses   15
Windows and Mirrors   21
The Big "6-0"   25
Some Assembly Required   31
Haikus   35
Black Path/White Path   39

THE MIND   43
Hard Time in the Big House   45
Midnight Online Poker   49
Occupational Hazards   55
Overqualified   61
Hearing Aid   67
Little Angels/Lying Dogs   71
Orchestra Seats   75
My Wife's Fortieth High School Reunion   79
Acquired Taste   83

THE BODY   89

    Adrenaline Junky/Cold Turkey   91

    15th Hole   95

    The Garden   99

    Galapagos   103

AUTHOR'S NOTES   106

A DISCUSSION OF THE POETRY   122

ABOUT THE AUTHOR   138

AUTHOR'S INTRODUCTION

The *endgame* is the final set of moves in a game of chess. Good players prepare for it throughout the game. It is often the most interesting part of the game because there are fewer pieces on the board and the range of motion is simpler, but the strategies can be very complex . . . and you are playing to win the game. And, of course, it matters *what* pieces are on the board and *where* they are.

Retirement often marks the beginning of the endgame for those who have worked for forty to fifty years—be it a job in the market economy, in government or the non-profit sectors, in the arts, the job of raising a family, or some combination. Some have prepared financially and physically, but, more importantly, mentally and spiritually . . . others have not. For some, retirement is welcomed. For others, it is dreaded and to be avoided.

It can be a very important milestone in our lives, which can present confusion and uncertainty or excitement and important new challenges. There are challenges to the Spirit, the Mind, and the Body.

These poems are loosely organized around these themes and, hopefully, may speak to some on this important phase of our game of life.

I must thank my wife and lifelong partner, Gayle, not yet retired as wife and mom, for her tireless, thoughtful, loving, and meticulous editing and support on this and other projects.

—Grady Means

The Spirit

" . . . how are your spirits today?"

One of the defining moments for many retirees is when they move from their predictable paychecks to fixed income,

. . . and, of course, "fixed income" may also reference the degree to which we can draw down on the lifelong investments we've made in our spiritual bank, as well as our financial resources,

. . . and, of course, our life itself is based on the "fixed income" of the number of hours allotted to each of us genetically to "do something," a reality that becomes even more clear to us in our retirement years.

. . .

Fixed Income

4:30 a.m. and I'm wide awake
Thinking, sweating, listening,
The distinctive middle-pitched tone
Of water running through pipes
Somewhere in the house.

4:30 a.m. is my special time
When I've always stared and worried
About parents, children, job, and retirement,
Cancer, death, marriage, or some slight
At the office or the dinner table.

My ears are very finely tuned
For that sort of thing.
The loose shutter, the expanding
Joints of the ductwork,
Doors opening and closing.

Drip, Drip, Drip
I have filled our rooftop tank
With financial mysteries . . .
401(K)s, defined benefits, savings,
Bond ladders, mutual funds . . .
And its magic must now be an engine that
Runs forever.

In my country, the rains have stopped
And will never come again
And so I go up
To measure the water level
Every day.

I worry that our plumbing is leaking
Someone left a faucet dripping
Or a toilet is stuck
And my home's organ pipes
Play a sonata of loss . . .
Something that I overlooked . . .
Or that broke in the night.

Drip, drip, worry, worry
The water runs out and we die.

So I creep up to the attic in the dark
And crawl out onto the roof
And climb the ladder on the water tank
Moonlight reflects off of the pool of water
And, as I stare down at the silver surface,
My glowing computer screen tells me that we are fine.

We often find ourselves older than we feel. Often, retirees are just not sure how they got so old on the outside so quickly. They are often in denial.

Then life comes along.

"Sir"

I had been surfing for about an hour
And I admit that I was a bit winded
Short gray hair and close-cropped beard
Betraying me to the surf lineup

I paddled in and caught a nice wave
Popping up slow, my balance a tilting windmill
But I was surfing, sliding fast down the wave
The unique rush of bonding with strong nature

I cut right, my back to the wave
And heard it crashing around me
The foam catching my board from the side
I was moving fast

I paddled back out to the line
And caught the smile of a thirty-year-old girl
I smiled back and turned my board
And sat up straight

We paddled for a wave together
And caught it, our boards sliding down the face
Side by side, we bonded briefly
in excitement and fear, heading into the beach

We surfed to the beach together
On the beach she rushed up to catch me
Tall and blonde and young
Mirror of my youth in a tight black wetsuit

"*Sir*," she said . . . my forced smile of sixty-five years
"You're killing me," I laughed
"No, No—You're an *inspiration*," she said
Three knives of frozen seawater through my heart

Many fear retirement because they may be at a loss without the drumbeat of their daily work schedule—phone calls, emails, meetings, tasks to complete, places to go.

Many become so defined by job, title, and schedule that they fear getting lost in retirement.

Fogged In

Every year in the fall, the tides shift
And come from the Northwest
Pushing away the warm surface water
Further south from our beaches

Deep cold water surges upward
From the sea bottom
To meet the warm air of autumn
And a cool creeping fog
Emerges ghostly from the waves and floats
Landward over our town

I've stopped "working" and
The warm wind of my career
Is suddenly hit with cold depths of
Age and solitude

And a fog has begun to creep out
From memories and idleness
And I feel around blindly
For the path no longer paved

I was a job and a title
A schedule of meetings and appointments
And due dates. And now?
Make-work to fill the day

And I find myself on soft ground
Becoming a swelling frigid sea
And I am vapor cold and blind
Fading to gray and lost

Most people have a collection of "life witnesses," accumulated over the years, against whom we measure ourselves or look to for validation. These may be school or job friends or rivals, mentors, parents or siblings, lovers, or others by whom we reference our lives. They may be people who know what we went through or what we achieved, or they may be people we've always wanted to prove something to. They keep the chronicles and archives of our lives. Many of these people, perhaps most, may not even know they play that role for us.

As we age and retire, our witnesses begin to die, and, as they do, a part of our lives is forgotten or permanently remains unsettled. While we may be somewhat liberated, a part of us dies with each of them . . . they are the keepers of our flame and are part of us.

Witnesses

They've followed me forever
I hear them coming
My life's shadows
Have my number, know me
But don't know that they are me

I know them all distinctly
Perhaps not as they are
But as I saw them
Maybe what they really were
Was just a part of me

As they prowl around
In the alleys of my memories
My stories change, and that's okay
It is more real
As they become me

They've never thought about it
I would guess
Or they would call or visit
They see it more casually
Never caring that they're me

They're right in my face
I see all the details
As they rush up to me
When I least expect it
They've no idea they're here

Marching as a group
They can't see me or each other
My little regiment of strangers
Phantoms and Shadows
Linked arm in arm with me

Some are right on my heels
Others lay way back
Some living with me
Others tracked by rumor
Never sensing that they are me

I may scan the paper
Or track them on a screen
Maybe I should call them
But that would be strange
The chaos of my brain invading them

To me familiarity
To them a cool distance
Across the cosmos and the years
At best a faded memory
But always haunting me

My Life's Blind Accountants
Keeping score for me
From whence I came
To where I go
Keepers of my Treasury

Friends and Rivals
Mentors and Critics
Building the JumboTron
Of points and errors
And flashing the final score

Our only real monument
Harder than stone or bronze
A life etched in rings
Built to confine us
And truly define us

Wife and Children
Father, Mother, Brother, Sister
Neighbors and Bank Tellers
Marking small and large
In my book of accounts

They are my romantic
Successes
But more likely
Failures
Painting my memories
In Black, and White, and Shades of Gray

I can recall them clearly
Gestures, words
Slights in full color
Unexpected kindness somewhat gray
Life's odd connections and pictures
As they made the film of me

They are my life's witnesses
And without them
My life has less meaning
Or driving force
For as a group, they are me

I live to show them What
I've done and accomplished
I shout to them
You were right, you were wrong
That they knew, or didn't know at all

And now they start to disappear
Wait! You'll never know
And never really cared
And I begin to disappear
As each erases a part of me

My house is now on fire
Scrapbooks and letters
Going up in flames
A futile struggle
To rescue any scraps

And so they all die and are gone
And never knew the role
They played in my little drama
As they leave, the act completes
And the houselights go up

Love others as yourself
It's a curious idea
Especially when you are them
And they don't know
They are you

It's a strange idea
To love a God who wrote your play
And hired the cast
And yet life's witnesses are you
And knowing that is loving God

As we face retirement and move to our next role in life, many feel like they will go crazy, living with only their own thoughts and memories. Many may decide to "work till they die." They worry about being confined and cooped up in retirement and sometimes fail to see the huge new opportunities that lie within their imagination.

Still others find themselves confined and defined by their past, what they have done, stuff they have accumulated, memories of the past . . . and it often keeps them for moving on, living in the present, tackling new adventures, and living their lives.

Windows and Mirrors

I look out the window
At vast oceans with mystery beneath
And dark forests with hidden tales
And huge mountains that challenge
And broad deserts to cross

Out my window there are huge cities
With stories behind each window
And rolling country hills and farms
With flowers and animals and
Fields in which to run

But my house is shrinking
And my windows have become
mirrors

And my views have been replaced
By my small room
My face looking back at me
And I see the home that I have built

It is filled with little treasures
I have collected along my way
Pictures of my travels and friends
Little plaques and awards

It contains many stories
But few mysteries
And little promise of adventure

But I break the mirror
And see outside again
And I am trapped
By mirror or glass no more

I smell the sea
And the fragrance of the sage
I hear the wind
And the noisy sounds of life

So I slip though the open gap
And once again find the oceans
The forests and the cities
And run in the fields

Numbers make a huge impact on our lives, and one of those is 60. As we pass that number, we begin to feel that a milestone has been reached that leads to the last journey of our lives. For a few, it is liberating and calls on them to apply their experience and "wisdom" to new adventures and finding serenity. For others, it is the starting gun for the last slow trudge toward oblivion.

For my money, it is a great number, and, in that spirit, I'd like to offer a toast to the Big "6-0."

The BIG "6-0"

Happy 60th Birthday!!
Play the music, sing the song
Balloons and presents
Big smile now!! Great!! Good job!!
You're so dead!!

"6-0"—the "0" a millstone around our neck
The "6" life's weighted hook that drags us to the very bottom
Of the pool, muddy sediment without sentiment
The mark of mortality, the downhill slope
Perhaps the "6" a swirl, a vortex
The waterslide to the 0-blivion

What is this "6-0"?
What does it mean?
What does it say?
Can you hear it?

That "6"
A rocking chair, soft cushion
We sit on it and rock
And stare into that "0"
That oval mirror that reflects . . . what?
Us, our wrinkles, the look in our eye

No Nostradamus mirror this
No eye into the future
No coming adventures and challenges
To confront and conquer
Just scratched and broken glass

Rocking and looking into the mirror
The rearview picture of our lives
Living in the past, we look and see back to our
Life's story around us
Ravages of age on our faces and bodies

We must get up and put on some makeup
Press out those wrinkles
If we can get out of this chair
Honest mirror holds our gaze

Maybe if we keep working
Keep living that life in the mirror
We will stay young
And still be able to run

Oh, break that mirror!

This "6" is not a chair at all, but a fishing pole
And the "0" a pond that we can finally cast into
And pull out the big trout
That has been waiting for us all these years

Or maybe that "6" is our new driver
That "0" a high-compression golf ball
That we have wanted to really smack
For years

Or maybe that "6" is our putter
And that "0" is the hole
That we have ranged far and wide to find
To "plunk" into in the soft, wet turf

Ughhh! No! We reject that life!
I'll sit on the grass a while longer, thank you
Rather than drop into a hole
And lie below

Reject
The makeup, the forever young
The looking back, the clinging
Working till we die

NO—that "6" is a spring
Which we have coiled tightly for years
With our dues, paid dearly, our wisdom
And certainly some grace

And that "0"
A magic portal
That can only be found with age
And experience

And so we climb up on our spring
And test it lightly
And then we let it
Spring us forward

Through the "0"
Flying through the portal
Where we find a new world
A new spirit, an entirely new life
No yoke, no anchor, no mirror
Forming "6"s into wings . . . and we fly

Wisdom? Experience? Things accomplished? Are we satisfied with our lives? If we are our life's engineers, what did we build? They say, "man plans, God laughs." Fair enough. Then wisdom must be in the realm of doing the best we can and being able to recognize that whatever we did was okay. It is way beyond resignation. Perhaps true wisdom is in trying hard and being contented, and maybe amused, with the result.

Some Assembly Required

Clink, scratch, scratch
Roll, roll, hum
Plunk, ping, ping
Bam, bounce, bounce
Bonk

Rube Goldberg designed my life
And sent me this big contraption
In pieces, regular mail, COD
A cardboard box, clearly stamped
"Some assembly required"

The directions weren't
Completely clear
And I didn't have all
The tools
I needed

But I never read directions
Anyway
So I put it all together
And here it is
I guess

And it seems to work
Sort of
The little balls roll
Down the chutes and over the rails
The kickers kick, the levers lever

The track is a great color of orange,
A turquoise umbrella turns above,
Chutes of purple and white stripes
The ball is red and black marble
And a light flashes at the end.

Clunk, and off the ball goes
It falls off metal cliffs
Drops on teeter-totters
Moves the fan blades
And plunks onto new rails

But what does it do?
Where is it going?
When it gets there,
How do I know
That's where it was supposed to go?

Did I put it together
Right?
Well, it does something
And things seem to move
And get to the end . . . I guess.

Clink, Thunk
Roll, roll, roll
Creak, whoosh, bam
Whomp, bing, bing, roll, roll
Crack, bonk, beep, beep, beep
What does it all mean?

When I look at it now
It's not what I expected at all
Not the smooth long rush
To the finish
But a lot of starts, stops
Turns and loops

I never expected it
To glow in the dark
And jump from one track
To another
And have a funny tune.
Is it important?

But then I start it up
And it looks pretty cool to me
And I guess that's all that matters
Did Rube have a plan?
I don't really care, I like it.

Finally, with this vast amount of "wisdom" we've accumulated, what can we say about life?
It's probably best to keep this part very simple.

Haikus

People are the same.

You me, me you too
Can you see a difference?
Our true God is blind

Love all people as ourselves.

People are scary
Different, strange, and foreign
Be brave; love them all

Be kind to everyone.

One beautiful house
If the door is ever closed
God is not there

Accepting our spirits and loving others is loving God.

Life through many years
A vessel to fill with light
Light is God and you

It is never about doctrine, rules, and ritual. God and our spiritual lives are not bound by time and space.

I'm not eternal
I am timeless and placeless
Now, not forever

Prayer is about opening, not asking.

Pray for God to speak
But do not ask for prizes
God does not listen

Listen to and be moved by the spirit.

Life's long river flows
God gives us water to drink
Some seeds crack and grow

And finally:

Rumi said it well
Listen to your spirit's voice
Find and speak the truth

Getting older and retiring can often cut loose our moorings. In addition to losing our anchors of job and income, we also begin to more fully sense our mortality and are forced to test the logic and reasonableness of our core beliefs—to see if they are really strong enough to take us to the edge of oblivion.

It is at this point that we can chose between the paths of hope and joy . . . or despair and futility.

Black Path/White Path

Half awake, early morning haze
Heart beating, mildly sweating
On the Black Path
Where the air is very cold

I walk the endless field
Darkening every step
As twilight fades
And I am lost

Thinking Hemingway/shotguns
Memories fading gray,
No strength to hunt or fish
Life's muse, my time gone

Gods dead or dying
Compass spinning on its axis
No longer finding true north
Black crows fill the air

Awake, I am all alone
With the chill of oblivion
Seeing that what I thought
Was light, was darkness

I will soon be gone and be no more
In the ground and dust
My pictures will be burned
My face forgotten

So I must end it all
And no longer be tortured
And no longer scream out
To deaf Time

But I feel the lightest touch
And I am steered onto
The White Path
Which is always there

I see my way across this field
With a bright torch
That leads my march
Toward the growing line of dawn

Thinking now of youthening
Merlin and mystic signs
Of the world we cannot see
But our spirits guide us to

The sound of the Water
The brush of the Wind
The warmth of Fire
And the smell of Earth and forest

A growing music
Rising from my soul
Causes me to dance
And sing

And I feel the light
And heat of human touch
The unexpected kindness, blinding flash of wit
Striking beauty and connection

All spirit shadows that insinuate
There is much more
And that I am one
With everyone

And I see that Clock,
Other's hope and faith, was but illusion
And I am neither old nor young
And do not care at all

All fear is pushed aside
And I surge with joy of life
In the priesthood of the spirit
We all sit down and smile at God

The Mind

". . . what are you thinking about today?"

Life has an interesting pacing. We work for many years and may raise a family. And during that period, we build our home. And collect, and fill it up. Many make their homes Monuments, others make them Museums, some are even Mausoleums to last forever. Most are overbuilt and overstuffed. And they often own us, rather than the other way around.

Then, suddenly, we retire, the kids are gone, and we are rattling around in our homes, which may begin to feel more like cell blocks than sanctuaries.

The question becomes whether we have built within ourselves, in our minds and spirits, over the years, a home that we can live in comfortably and happily, furnished with our own thoughts and ideas.

Hard Time In
The Big House

Bang goes the Gavel
thirty years behind bars
no time off for good behavior
no chance of parole

I looked around at my cell
7,500 square feet, fifteen rooms
five bedrooms, five baths
study and a bonus room

heated pool and spa
tennis court
massive front lawn
a circular drive

granite tops, Viking range
Brazilian cherry floors
a Steinway in the living room
We can comfortably seat twenty for dinner

a view of the 4th green
and the ocean in the distance
direct TV and wireless cable modem
high-speed internet

Turbo Carrera next to
the Harley
skis, surfboard, golf clubs,
road bike hanging in the
three-car garage

I'm rattling around
Checking for mail
Going online
Lots of Stuff
Slow Decay
A Crowded Warehouse
The walls of the cell close in

The guards give me jobs
to wile away the time

But I have the keys to the cell

Time is no enemy to me
It is my freedom
To begin to think the thoughts
And have the feelings
And find the Spirit

That I kept in a box for forty years

When I was young I thought and felt
But did not know what
And so I was taught to put it all
Away, and forget

And so I worked
And taught
And traveled
And built things
But now I am done
And can open my box again

And what I've found in it is a
Bigger House
That I will Live in Forever

Confronting modern isolation, electronic social networking has become a ubiquitous formula for connecting people.

From another perspective, it is a very weak form of communication and social attachment, and often a forum for exhibitionism and occasional sociopathic behavior.

Retirement may often be isolating, and the question arises as to whether electronic social networks help or hurt.

Hey, whatever works! Some days, I may place my bet on time in the company of strangers.

Midnight Online Poker

The game starts around 12:30 AM
Bruhaha from Sidney is signed on
JonnyBoy from Hong Kong
GoldenGirl from Munich
And RedskinsMan in Des Moines

The Asians seem a little clever
Midwest breeds the muscle men
The Germans are pure porn
And the Aussies are wild
Stereotypes from my built-in speakers

Call me NoAccount
Jk, jk, my accounting firm past
With a little outlaw edge
Pretty clever handle
Or at least I think it's funny, lol

Our plastic clubhouse
Is a great place to meet
And we have pretty good conversations
About stupid plays
And gutless moves, and bad beats

The scratching sound of shuffling cards
And the thunk and clink of bets
Punctuates my dark and quiet room
And provides me some good company
From the backlit screen

And as I see the flush
Coming together
My heart starts racing
And my hand begins to shake a little
I'll go all in, and win

JonnyBoy took the bait
A fish rising on these two Kings
And the German is dead money
In hopes his straight comes together
As do I

As the pile of chips scrapes across to my name
Bruhaha says Nice Hand
In the coded nh
And I respond with ty
Although I think he deserves an f

I am with this group for hours
Betting, bluffing, winning, and losing
Getting the suck-out and bad beat
Starting to see how they think
And maybe how they feel

I imagine JonnyBoy as small and slight
RedskinsMan a truck driver
Bruhaha as a blond surfer
And I suspect GoldenGirl may even be
A Guy—those Germans

Nintendo NoFriendo
Was the old warning for our kids
Whom we taught to face life
And people head-on
In person, really living

But as I watch my table
Carefully
And bluff and fool
And win and lose Real Money and Pride
I wonder

There are certainly souls
Out there, 100,000 signed on now
And they are thinking and talking
And shaking and smiling
And finding many others

Am I alone . . . or not?
Am I wasting time . . . or not?
Is this any less real
Than the obligatory birthday call
To distant relatives?

Communicating by click and clear intent
Together by choice and not obligation
Or by word and look and contract
I wonder which is more real
Or not

As I log out
And sit down to read a
Very good novel
I cannot help but feel
That I've left a room of friends.

Many fear retirement because they feel they may be bored without the daily rhythm and stimulation of a job to provide activity and meaning. They are driven to create value as the world has defined it for them.

It may be that most should fear the opposite: that a job has provided artificial activity and "value" to us and it is important to break away from that to really build our spirits and understand our lives—that is, that there may be no real peace or salvation in life without enjoying our own company and ideas the most of all.

And retirement is our last chance.

I offer up a retiree's prayer for salvation.

Occupational Hazards

Childhood: a paean to the church of boredom
Ceaseless movement with learning
Becoming, playing, trying, succeeding, failing
Molding solitude into fantasy and invention
And into a person

I found diamonds
In the yard
And precious gold in cardboard boxes
And many secrets of the universe
As I smeared paint across my face

Unlearned Doctrines of the Stars and night sky
With everyone different and
No one different
A God that is a close friend
and playmate

Adult supervision
Fencing, organizing, socializing
Teaching, stifling
The child is a priest of life's
Great mysteries, casting out the demon schedule

But children are carefully taught
And learn to fear
And understand the differences
And to be organized and busy
And they forget the Scripture of the Spirit

And they no longer look up
At the limitless night sky
But look down at the earth
And get in line
And march to the tune they are taught

Life's amnesia helps us forget
And we learn more, and work
And raise a family and tend to
Many obligations and add value
To the world

Meetings and schedules
Trips and conversations
Golf and tennis dates and
Bills to pay
The compass and roadmap of our lives

Our God is Occupation
Not ocular, since we cannot see
Beyond the screen in front of us
But perhaps the cult
Of Busy

And so we cease to search
The skies
Or probe our souls
Our inbox is full of mail and meetings
Delivering the message of our new God

But—Crash
There are no meetings
There is no mail
The phone does not ring
The occupational army has left

Lost on the empty battlefield
An eerie silence
Takes hold in the mist and fog
And we grope our way toward friendly lines
That are not there

The action
Has moved on
And without rank or battalion
We look for new worlds
To occupy

And so you retire
To a world of boredom
And a fear of not adding value
To the world
And of no troops to lead

But as you cross the empty field
Try not to overlook the diamond mine
That you used to dig in as a child
Long forgotten, but still full
Of precious stones

Again don your priestly robes
And learn again the old magic
That helped you search the sky
And the inner secrets
Of your soul

And put aside the differences
That became the grid-map of your life
And meet the God that loves all
And the others all
With the same light

Stop, listen
Put down the mail and phone
Forget the schedule and the bills
Listen to the silence
And find yourself again

Amen

It is often said that most people spend a lifetime mastering the irrelevant.

One of the odd problems of retirement is how much we learn and know that we will never use again. We have spent a lifetime accumulating knowledge for our job and for raising a family and for life's various problems, and then, suddenly, we retire and may find that we have little use for all the knowledge and know-how we accumulated over many years. We can't sell it, and we may not even be able to give it away.

It makes you wonder whether it was worth the effort. It also makes you think about all those people with all that information that just grow old and die. Does a lot of important knowledge just disappear? Is it just a huge waste?

What is the point?

Overqualified

I have to say that
I know a lot
Of stuff
That I'd like to tell you

About running big companies
How the world really works
What will happen between countries
How people will act and behave

I can really help a lot of people
I know how to solve financial problems
How to start businesses
How to fix schools and hospitals
And cars and plumbing and broken furniture

When to change the oil and
Check the tires and replace the filters
In the car and the furnace and
How to mow the lawn and make the plants
Grow and look great

How to write books and
Deliver speeches
And give people hope and lead
Them to do great things

How to woo women
And raise kids and deal with
Difficult relatives or people at work
Or in other cars or the checkout line

And know when people are lying to you
Or trying to help you or
Want something from you or are a little
dangerous

How to get jobs and move up in companies
Or governments
How to avoid problems with banks
How to get mortgages and insurance
And arrange for gas and electricity and
Phone service

Lots of tricks; how to ride a motorcycle
And surf and snowboard and play the tin whistle
And sail a really big boat
And also win at poker, when to go all in

And I have great stories about
Our family and my jobs
And trips and people and Broadway shows
And really cool things I've seen

And I'd really like to share a lot of that
With you if you have any time
But I know you're really busy learning
This stuff for yourself and seeing things yourself

I just don't know what to do with all this stuff
If I don't have any need for it
And I can't seem to give it away
And nobody knows that I know
This stuff . . .

But wait . . . one other thing
I have learned in all these years
Is that we are all vessels
Carrying precious oils and other
Treasures

And much of our cargo may
Be delivered to eager traders
Who turn our simple silk and oil
Into unimaginable clothes and food

But our ships may also
Be caught by storms and sink
And our jars and chests may
Sit on the seabed for many years
Only to be rediscovered

And true value may be
In the making, in the using,
Or simply in the seeing
And imagining

Or the value of the cargo
May have been in the child watching
It being made, or
watching it loaded and shipped

Or in seeing how it weighted
Down the ship
And wondering what, or how,
Or why
And so the World's billions
In their cicadic rhythm
Appear, live, and die
And huge knowings die with them

But . . . maybe not . . .

Here we are
Matter and energy
Nothing created nor destroyed
But the glimmer of an idea
And the flicker of a candle that never blows out

One of the artifacts of getting older and retiring, losing titles and leading roles, with previous employers moving on and children starting their own lives, is that it is easy to imagine that people listen to you less. That your views are less important.

Wisdom and grace, of course, tell you that is wrong and that the power of your ideas and experience still carry a lot of weight, and yet, you may need a . . .

Hearing Aid

My hearing has always been acute
I only hear bad stuff, rarely good
The problem, the slight
The tone of voice
That insinuates the insult
The critique
That no one else seems to hear
Or understand
In quite the same way I do
I find the subtle
Undertone that conveys
An amplitude and frequency
That my tone-deaf
Friends can never hope to
Hear

As I get older, my hearing
Is even more finely tuned
And I hear whispers that
Escape notice for most
The low murmur
That tells me that my house
Is under siege, again
And I must prepare my army
To battle these
Quiet ninjas
Whose soft footsteps
Only belie their
Lethal intent

I call out to friends
To join me
But they are careless
To the threat and
To me
Perhaps they have gone totally deaf
Or crazy or both
And so I shout even louder
And they look up briefly
And smile
And continue talking

Kids will always be our children to us. Even when they grow up and have careers and families, we have great respect for them, but still see them as our "kids." That may get magnified when we retire.

Part of getting older is watching children growing up and thinking back on raising them, always questioning decisions and choices, but also clearly seeing yourself in them.

Little Angels/Lying Dogs

You can go ahead and say it . . .
I have No Clue
It's all so different,
You really don't need
To listen to me

The music and the talk
And the gadgets,
Hardware and software
I can't keep up

But you spend time
With me
And talk to me
And really try

And yet there are secrets
That you know
And your friends know
And I don't know

We went to bed early
We didn't drink
We don't smoke
We don't do any other stuff either

But actually I do know
I know it all because
I was you, sort of,
And I lied

I lied to live
To escape and
Create and build my house
Where I could learn
and grow

You are wonderful
Strange, exciting creatures
Very different, thank God, and yet
You are really me

We are witnessed and witness. On the same theme of Life's great drama, it is important to know when to leave the stage, retire, and go into the audience. Many try to continue to run the lives of those around them, long after it's time from them to gracefully withdraw and invite the next generation to take the stage.

Orchestra Seats

These are good seats
Right up front
I sit and cheer . . . or politely applaud
I don't want to distract
The young cast
Of this great play.

I've made a night of it,
My best clothes, new shoes
Double-check my tickets
Wonderful dinner
And now the show.

I love this play, wrote part of it myself
I know the storyline and most of the words
Act 1: Growing up, going to school
Act 2: Getting a job, having a family
Dreams, Disappointments, Surprises
Always been a classic.

Act 3 always needed work
Once again in rewrite
How to end the story well?
Comedy or tragedy?
Tough to close it up.

Must be a new Director though
Something has been added
Key parts have changed
I lean forward to shout out the lines
To help them get it right.

And as I start to rise and shout
"Don't do that . . . it won't work"
They do it and it does
And I sit back in my seat
And watch, a little puzzled.

It all looks, and sounds, and even smells
So differently from here
I see the whole thing
In such a broader way
I could never see from the stage.

Occasionally I'll lean over
And in sotto voce say . . . "I did it differently"
Or "Really good" or "That's not right"
And the actors shoot me a look
As I hum the music.

They used to cheer my acting
It was pretty good
I should be up there still
On the stage, giving my lines
And cleverly adding a little of my own.

I loved my audiences
There was no play without them
Their silent presence moved me on
And I soared on their approval
Schooled in their murmurs.

But now I sit here
In the comfortable seats
And play my next great role
Not on the stage, not on the marquee
Important nonetheless.

No longer acting in the play
I still drive the story forward
With no words or gestures
But not just scenery,
Sitting quietly and watching.

Reunions are part of the gauntlet of growing older and retiring. They are time to reminisce and renew lost friendships.

But make no mistake. For some, high school is forever and reunions are a blood sport. The scorecards are out and under scrutiny.

And it is a time to test who we really are.

My Wife's Fortieth High School Reunion

I have to be frank with you
I could not think of anything
I would have more preferred to dodge
Than My Wife's Fortieth High School Reunion

I had watched the work of preparation
With detachment and amusement
The excitement and anticipation
The yearbook, memories, and discoveries

I could only imagine
The high-pitched shrieks
Of old friends rushing
To greet one another

Each casting laser glances at the guys
Remembering classes, parties
Football games, couples, regrets
And the occasional backseat success or failure

The approach of ritual
Looks blending expectation
And trepidation and certain questions
Which have lingered for many years

With the instant appraisal of finely tuned radar
Fully armed and battle ready
Hug, Kiss, a lifelong blood sport
From saddle shoes to Jimmy Choos

You look just the same
I had a crush on you
Memories of all these people
Could all of this be true?

Nametags tell the life story
As they all squint for names to put with
The wizened faces morphing from the
Expectant pictures of youth

Different last names
That speak of choices made
Some leading to a life of peace
Others not, some *really* not

I saw the narrowed eyes
Of hunters
And the nervous eyes
Of prey

Some promoting life stories or resume
Of job and family, illness and pain
Others approaching fully unarmed
Without story or guile

And our life's accountants
Working overtime to run the numbers
And total the score from the beginning of the race
Till now

But then I began to see
The human integrity in all of this
The dig for true foundations
And a perspective on each life

I watched it all and as I did
I saw mirrors of my wife
Lighting darkened corners
And shining on a cool young girl

And I came to know that
I had formed a mirror too
The choices made, the victories won
The woman she had become

And I came away as I always do
When forced to see her through a new lens,
More in love, more alive
And perhaps a better person

Finally, during retirement, as you spend more time together, your most important relationship with your spouse needs to be resolved. Roles change dramatically from the period of working and raising a family to the period of living together in retirement.

It can magnify problems that have been covered over by life and activity . . . or it can grow and become more wonderful.

Acquired Taste

We've been working on this little motor
For nearly thirty years
Connecting the wires
Putting in the resistors
Checking the Capacitors

We have overloaded this little motor
Many times
Too much power
Too much Resistance
Reverse polarity

We made the little engine Smoke
Wires got crossed
Things became disconnected
Fuses blew, Sparks flew
And it shorted out

Be we kept working on it
And soldered it
Back together
And reconnected the wires
And tinkered with the power supply

And over the years
It started to run smoother
And smoother
And now it just hums along
And you can barely hear it

The key feature of design
Was to balance
The positive and negative charges
Which created the right tension
To make the turbine spin

On off, on off
Push pull, push pull
Plus minus, plus minus
Turning the magnet off and on
To complete the circuit

Binary math
The physics of human relations
The tension and attraction
The yin and yang
Of two equal and opposite poles

The negative moves the positive
And then a little rest
And then a little more juice
And the motor runs and runs

There is always
A little pain
But as with Kafka's strange machines
After a long time
The pain creates the hidden pleasure

Alternating tension
If the energy is all positive
Or all negative
The motor just sits there
Static with the smell of smoke

Balanced power
If one of the poles
Pulls too hard
It begins to vibrate, out of control
And flies apart

So my wife and I
Argue over many things
And she rarely misses an opportunity
To point out areas for
Self-improvement

And I help her out
On social graces and
Raising kids
Her driving, of course,
And her "flawless" bookkeeping

We have called each other
Every name in the book
In that vast contradiction
That is the foreplay
Of love

But we also see
The cool idea, the special look
And that certain grace
The knowing consideration
And the quiet touch of support

And the push
Becomes the pull
Of human attraction and fascination
That can run for a lifetime
And more

And we have learned to
Do this dance with a certain rhythm
That keeps the motor moving
Smoothly along
Smoother and Smoother each Year

And as with many things
That are very good for you
But not so attractive at first taste
You need to season it just right
And acquire the palate for it

And only if you cook it
Long enough
You find that after many years
Resistance and tension reach a balance
That tastes really good and keeps love alive

Many grow old
With a hope for bland serenity
But life's great banquet is hardier fare
And the best courses have a certain bite
With a dessert worth waiting for.

Body

". . . how are you feeling today?"

When we retire, the pace of our days may change a lot, from early alarms, endless calls at home, and trips to the airport to a more leisurely pace.

That may take a little getting used to and may actually be tough on the body.

Adrenaline Junky/
Cold Turkey

For the last 50 years
I have been training
For the Olympics
Look out

30 minutes of cardio
20 minutes on the weights
10 laps in the pool
Quick sauna and hot tub
Dinner meeting, single malt please

Resting heart rate 52
Blood pressure 120/70
Total cholesterol 170
Eternal life is here
I only need 5 hours of sleep

Staff meeting, 7:30 a.m.
Board convenes at 9
Lunch and speech at 12:15
Car will be here at 4
7 p.m. flight to New York

Triple latte please
I'm completely wired
I can do this forever—wait!
Full stop, face-plant, brick wall,
I've retired

Alarm clock anxiety
5 a.m. or 10 a.m.
no meetings, no calls,
no speeches, no flights
no boards, dead silence

The race is over
And I have won
The Porsche is tuned and ready,
And sitting in the garage

And I Refuse to Stop,
Run or die
Tick tock
Time is wasting
Got to get moving

The power of my system surges
Like a huge wave looking
For a beach to crash on
But finding only an endless ocean

*Of course, what would retirement be without golf…
or at least the image and metaphor of golf?*

15th Hole

Ah, the 15th
The "old man's hole"
Not as you would think
A short par 3
With a short chip to the green

Nor an easy
Straight par 4
With a broad green fairway
And few traps or hazards
To catch the errant shot

No, the 15th is a long par 5
Longest hole on the course
Fairway a green bobsled chute
And a gauntlet of sand and water
To consume the careless shot

The 15th green a citadel
The Devil's Tower
Cloaked in green velvet
Converting 4s into 7s
In chipping and putting alchemy

The exuberance of youth
is often jailed
with a trip to the woods
a swim in the pond
or a fruitless search in weeds

To the slow and steady
The straight but short
The white orb perched and prized
In plain sight, not out of sight
Proudly to be pummeled on

And so we march up
To the green
My short chip up to the green
The youth lost in a sandstorm
Lying 4, lying 5

My putt for par
Clunking in
The youthful putt rushes past
And declares the lowly
Turtle won

Pretty clear to anyone
Who sees the game for what it is
But it seems a lot less fun
Than belting balls long
An endless search for falling stars

But I have little time
Or stroke for that
And so I play a stolid game
Card a par, take their money
And go home

A lot of life is closing well
Putting a lifetime of lessons
In the bag, to strike the ball
With patience
And pass some wisdom on

We finish our adventure
The ball glides smoothly across the green
Hesitates on the edge of the hole
Falls into the earth, "clunk"
And I exult upon the grass, not yet under it

. . . and, if there is a game as popular as golf among retirees that anyone can play, it is the game of "symptoms" . . .

The Garden

I walk in my old garden
Moss-covered stone walls
Neat rows of flowers and herbs
Planted over the years

And everything seems to be in bloom
The garden is a place of beauty,
And death, and harvest
A carousel of fruit and compost

Mushrooms are in bloom
With little polyps popping out everywhere
Little pink balloons that may burst and spread tiny
seeds across
The yard if the gardener doesn't harvest them

And mold is growing from overwatering
And has created a sticky mess in the pipes
To plug things up or just break loose
And clog the valves and plumbing

And some of the trees
Have grown tall
And have become a little old
And dry and brittle over the years

But it is the flowers that
Glorify this garden
Hallelujah, the brightly colored headscarves
Reflect the inner soul that never dies

The scarf ladies bloom
Beautiful petals in a spectrum of color
Batik, paisley, silk, cotton
Designer or not, but never common

The river of life
Air, food, water, earth, and light
Eat, breathe, and warm themselves
Covered in water diamonds

Growth and color masks the war
Bright pennants trumpeting the hopeless clash
The inevitability,
The crown of death

Crowns covering white stems and faces
Large eyes locked in fear and confusion
Agonies of death, but shields of hope
Covered in glory, turning to dust

Measure of the times, they cover the garden
There are more flowers these days
More seeds are strewn across this
Garden and those of my neighbors

And autumn comes and
The bracing winds blow the winged seeds
Bright flags looping away across the land
And cancer's flowers are asleep

Retirement is a serious game ... a battle to the death. It is a point in time where we make a choice to live or die. It is a time when we must adapt to a jolting change in our life's frame of reference.

We must decide how we think, how we view life, and how we really view the spirit, God, and the ultimate purpose of our life. It is our last chance to put our affairs in order.

It is Darwinian.

Galapagos

I've come to this dry island for many years
It doesn't look like much
But this is where it all happens!
I take my seat in the bleachers and await
The grand parade.

And here they come!
Tortoises, Finches, Iguanas,
And Boobies
They march by proudly
Although not in very good order

Around and around the island they march
And each time they pass
The bells in the massive clock tower
Rising in the center of the island
Toll their passing

The Old Man sitting on the tower
Waves as they pass
And as they nod to Him in reverence
I see the slightest twinkle in His eye
Just for an instant

My job is to mark the changes
In Shell, Beak, Color, Size
The narrative
That forever denotes "life"
Within each creature

I take very careful notes in my book,
How they've changed
Some young, some old
How they march, who is out of line
The marks they leave in the sand

The sun shines bright and warm
And the passing creatures seem to
Soak it in to live
Phototropic to the light
Of survival and necessity

But look! When they pass
I see the same small twinkle
From each creature, exactly the same
Just for the slightest instant
It touches my eye and it's gone

And when I close my eyes
I cannot see the island
And the clock and Old Man are not there
I hear no bells
But the shadow of the twinkle stays

And I see there are no changes at all
No young, no old
No marks in the sand
That change is life's fantasy
And history has made me blind

I was fooled
As my mind weaved a story
And created a clock and compass and map
Of a time and place of dreams
And measured all the land

I see that Timelessness
Is not forever
And Placelessness
Is not eternal
And Change is not

So I close my book
And open my eyes
And see that I am neither young
Nor old, no story, no narrative,

And I need not march at all.

AUTHOR'S NOTES

Retirement is one of modern life's most important milestones, and it can be enormously disorienting for many. One day you're part of an army of working people, with a schedule and set of tasks; the next day you're completely cut loose, with no place you really need to go and nothing you really need to do. One day you move with clear purpose; the next day is a little murky.

Many surprising changes, which most people are unprepared for, come together and hit us all at once. It is very different from the structure of school or work. We are suddenly playing a role in a Sartre play in which there is very little action, it is quiet, and everyone is waiting for us to deliver our lines . . . except that someone forgot to give us the script. We are forced into a lot of improvisation.

And there is just not much written about this huge transition that is retirement. Of course, there are plenty of financial strategy books, fitness and health guides, and many joke books about retiring, but there is not much in the literature at all about what it actually *feels like* to retire or *how* to retire from a mental or spiritual perspective.

So, I thought I'd try to *process* this most interesting process of turning sixty-five and retiring and write about it, and poetry emerged as the best medium. And, in my process, I came to more fully appreciate why this was such a very important transition in life, and that it is rich, but largely untilled, soil for philosophy and the rhythm of verse.

To put it in perspective, when we turn sixty-five and retire, modern actuarial tables tell us that we have the last quarter to third of our lives still to lead—perhaps twenty or thirty years—so much time to create things, see things, think about things, spend more time with family and friends, and maybe even apply the knowledge and "wisdom" accumulated over our first sixty to sixty-five years.

Of course, to many it looks like they're entering a dark cave. In the pitch darkness, they can only hear the Tick, Tock, Tick, Tock, 10,950, 10,949, 10,948, as their final days tick off and they have really no idea what to do. Some may feel like they need to hurry to get a number of things done before it is too late. Others may feel that the rapidly approaching horizon makes any new and large projects pointless.

To be honest, there are still a huge number of days left, and it really is a little too dramatic to think of it as a boring, final trudge toward the shores of oblivion. But if that's right, what, then, is it?

People often talk about aging as a narrative of loss, and there are certainly elements of that. We slow down a little, we are regarded as a little less capable than the younger and more nimble, some friends die, there are a few more aches and pains. But, not to be too banal, it is also a time of huge opportunity.

I describe this period as the ***endgame***—a term I use in a very optimistic and positive way.

The *endgame* in chess is the decisive set of moves in a long match, the exciting climax that determines the final outcome. The *endgame* is often the most important part of the game. It is not necessarily a short part of the game. It may not matter who won the opening moves or the tactical middle game. It often doesn't matter who has the most pieces on the board . . . although it *is* important to have the right pieces . . . in the right places. Entering the endgame is not really the end—it is the beginning of a conclusive and great struggle to win the game . . . although "winning" may be a misnomer in the game of life, since we all will wind up in exactly the same place, and, frankly, are all forgotten soon enough. Life for everyone at any stage is about life, and monuments and museums turn to dust in a relatively short time.

So, if it's not about finishing our shrines, or even about our last great hurrah or surge of missed recreation, what is our endgame about?

In chess, endgame strategies must be focused. Since there are fewer pieces to manage on the board, and the range of motion is far more limited, and the board seems a lot smaller—perhaps less important and interesting— than before, we need a very different approach.

In our life's endgame, we compete without job titles, with less perceived status, with fewer economic and family responsibilities, with fewer daily obligations. But it need not be a time when we feel trapped or cornered like the lonely King on the chessboard, clunking along a square at a time, trying to stay away from the faster and nimbler (younger?) rooks, knights, and bishops.

It may, in fact, be a time to return to more subtle and simple ideas (although, as a Buddhist might point out, "simple" can sometimes be very complicated). It may be a time when we abandon the false and wooden gods of "forever young" or "work until I die" and find our real spirit in getting to know ourselves and using our time in ways that are truly satisfying. It may be a time of truth and willpower—of patience and concentration.

The stakes may appear much lower during this phase; it is a slow withdrawal; we are "retiring." But, actually, the stakes are much higher than they have ever been—it is a final, climactic phase in which we are competing for a true claim on our ourselves, a claim no longer fully held or dominated by job or raising a family. And the competition may be fierce because we are just "competing" with ourselves, using all that we have learned over a lifetime.

It is the period when we decide if we have real integrity, and if we can live with ourselves. It is a great time to decide, once and for all, what we really think, what we know, and what we believe, and be brave enough to defend it to ourselves and to others. At this stage, there is no point in leaving anything on the table. As some philosopher once said, if you have integrity, you never need to worry about reputation. At the stage of retirement, we should have enough integrity that we really don't care what others think; we should adopt a real honesty about what we think and who we are, and live according to our real values. And, with that level of self-awareness, it may be a time to leave something very real, something truly valuable, but intangible, behind, and to "pay it forward," as they say.

Said another way, retirement is really simple: a point in our lives during which we decide to live or to die (physically,

mentally, spiritually), and to complete the job of living or
to throw in our cards. It is a period of testing—a determi-
nation of how much perspective and personal strength we
have developed over the years. It is a period of honesty—
it determines whether we are comfortable with our own
company in the "spiritual" or mental home we have built
over the years. It tests whether we have discovered what it
really means to "be productive" or "create value." It can be
the most interesting and exhilarating period of our life, or
it can be a period of losing our bearings, confusion, and
depression. We can be busy and challenged, or we can be
bored and lost. We can strengthen our spirit, or we can
try to distract ourselves into numbness with pointless oc-
cupation and recreation. It can be renewal and rejuvena-
tion, or it can be hermetically sealed doom. It can be full
of voices and laughter (even if we are alone), or it can be
silent (even if we are surrounded by noisy people). It can
be the most rewarding part of our life, or it can be sterile
and dead. It is an oddly simple choice we all must make.

It is often called the Golden Years, but gold is not sup-
posed to tarnish, and our bankers, and lawyers, and doc-
tors, and newly found lobbying and insurance advisors at
AARP will be quick to tell us that we are in a perilous pas-
sage and may be sinking fast. So, we find ourselves armed
and hopeful with IRAs and revocable trusts, and a cabinet
full of statins and Omega-3, and with a new appreciation
for the copay rules of Medicare and Part B, not to men-
tion the value of long-term care insurance and hospice.

Many people look forward to retiring. They may have
found themselves in a spiritually draining occupation that

is rapidly marginalizing them. Or they simply may anticipate new opportunities.

They plan for their financial future and carefully analyze their future sources of cash flow.

They plan their "life strategy" and move to an attractive location (sun, low taxes, low cost of living, interesting recreation, or other retirees to keep them company).

They allow for keeping themselves busy with new business ventures, new hobbies, travel, recreational interests. But those can never match the intensity of a lifelong job and raising a family, and they can never fill the time in the same way.

They commit to certain approaches to physical fitness and health. And these may become objectives in themselves . . . but giving a short extension to a shortening life can be an obviously futile task, if that is the only objective.

And all of this may work for some, for a time. But, for many, it entirely misses the point. It may be a new trap— the *time* trap. What *should* you do with your time?

In this you-are-what-you-do era, retirement is never just about quitting work, receiving retirement benefits, living off of savings, or finding some new hobbies. It is a fundamental change of personal identity and spiritual energy. We must either redefine who we are at the most fundamental levels or we will be lost, wither and expire with alarming speed. For each who feels liberated, there are many more who hear a death sentence.

For forty years or more, their entire identity has been consumed by efficient use of time: their work, its schedules

and deadlines, its meetings, its job titles, the growing re-
sume, the noise, and the home, which has become a mu-
seum or a warehouse of "assets." Professional success has
been the drumbeat and rhythm of their days. The answer
to the question "Who are you?" is often answered by "I
am the vice president of . . ." The premier cocktail party
question "And what do *you* do?" is painful to answer with
"Nothing; I'm retired." The standard refrain of "You're so
lucky" can be simultaneously translated into "You're so
dead" or "You must be so bored." It is very easy in this
stage of life to hear the question "What do you do?" as
"Why don't you do something useful with your time?"
Tick, Tock, Tick, Tock.

"What are you?" becomes "Why are you?"—obviously
not a very promising question.

We all should probably ask ourselves: how many layers
does our identity have? . . . do they go well beyond job
and family? . . . and do we have a map to access them?

Some may try to avoid all of these questions by not
changing at all. Even if they have the resources to retire,
they may decide to "work till they drop" and "die with
their boots on." And they may miss the huge opportunity
for the spiritual renewal that change and retirement and
having a lot more "free time" may offer. (The value of
time, perceived by most to be a dwindling commodity,
is, of course, a leitmotif for the entire discussion and the
poems. The ultra-philosophical or religious may perceive
that if we are "timeless" spirits, the *price* and *value* of time
is a profound question, a thought touched upon lightly in
some of the poems.)

Some may choose to engage in a lot more recreation, to do the things that they never had time for when they were working. But recreation may soon turn out to be a little "empty" and unproductive and a less and less satisfying distraction.

Some may choose to focus their efforts on social problems or charity work. And that may lead to spiritual renewal and purpose. Or, it may simply represent a new set of titles, tasks, and schedules. Even worse, it may make them more self-satisfied, self-righteous, or even evangelical—all spiritually corrosive.

Others may try to spend time in a more reflective mode. When the number of days ahead appears to be far less than the number of days behind, it puts a premium on putting how we use our time in proper perspective. What is really worth my time? What do I really have time to get accomplished? Will I have the health and energy for a major new project? Is maintaining my health and energy a sufficient project in itself? Do I need to find a way to make more money? But even that may have a time trap, as the growing perception of a shortening time horizon may even discourage some from tackling anything at all—a bug trapped in amber for eternity. Or, to paraphrase a previous poet: *The sands of time are covered with the bleached bones of those who hesitated, and, while waiting, died.*

People often live in the past and worry about the future. But the past is something we can't change and the future is something that we can't really control. As all philosophers will point out, the key is to be in (and appreciate) the *now*. Jesuits, Buddhists, and many other spiritual and philosophical disciplines concentrate on "being here, in the now." When we're working, there is often a pretty intense *now*—meetings, schedules, stuff we need to work on, now. The problem is that, when we retire, the now is not so clear—what do we want to do? So many retirees live even more intensely in the past and endlessly re-tell old stories. And, at the same time, many retirees live with even more worry about the future, and are eager to share their anxieties with those around them. Both are losing strategies.

And, so, we are caught in a Darwinian puzzle—our roles have changed, many of our skills are no longer needed, we have a significant portion of our lives to still live, we must adapt quickly or die.

For a moment, time stands still and it is really quiet. In one day, the biological balance of the world and the rules of life completely change. The simple decision on setting the alarm clock, which had been regulated by school and work schedules for more than forty years, suddenly presents a dilemma—wake up at 5 a.m. with no place to go, or wake up at 10 a.m. and feel like the day is half gone?

We quit adrenaline-driven days and suddenly go cold turkey, and are confronted with unfamiliar choices and the new pressure of *less pressure*. Adrenaline addiction may be a particularly bad habit for the future.

In a moment, the familiar chaos of work and schedules and urgent deadlines is replaced by silence. If you lived for work, you have a problem.

The phone does not ring.

You've got no mail.

You've got no game . . . or so it would seem if you apply your previous life measures.

If you lived for family, you have a problem. Kids are busy and have their own lives that you should not impose upon.

If you lived for prestige, you have a problem. You have no title.

It may be that one reason wives generally outlive their husbands, often by decades, is that they have in place a set of layers and networks and systems that have nothing to do with a job that terminates abruptly with retirement. For many wives, when children leave the house, it frees them up to further develop their core networks and interests in a way that is very different from husbands leaving an all-consuming job. It is very different than the adrenaline junky hitting the wall.

If you lived to compete, you have a problem. The opportunities for competition may have been reduced to golf, starting a new business, or adventure travel, and breaks heal more slowly at this age.

Your life's yardsticks begin to disappear. For many, life is *always* high school, and our *lifelong life witnesses* (those who knew us when we were young and awkward, when we first started to work, when we first gained life's insights in school or our professions, when we first experimented with love and romance—or at least fantasized about it, when we first took on our new challenges) begin to die. We may have not talked to them for decades, but they are always the somewhat warped and splintered yardsticks of our lives, and we often think of them as the people who can take the true measure of what we've become. As our witnesses disappear, their testimony disappears forever, and large chunks of our lives disappear with them. It becomes the silent death of our life story that no one will ever hear.

In any case, we go through huge changes whether we want to or not. We have important decisions to make.

So, what to do? These poems attempt to frame this question, provide some perspective, and provide some hints at the solution.

And, of course, all of this is a good and healthy process. We should not live in the past. A needed weeding of our garden that allows new growth is not loss, but opportunity. Without weeding, parts of our old life grow over us and we are trapped in the endless reminiscing and retelling of old stories of school or work. Similarly, any weeding must be accompanied with new seeding or it creates a desert.

Life has been and should continue to be a process—a process through which we have become aware, learned, practiced, succeeded or failed, learned more, tried again, and developed perspective and perhaps some wisdom. And retirement is no different. It is not a line in the sand, but rather another step in the process of our life. And we must continue to challenge ourselves to learn, to adapt, and to try.

It is an act of the spirit and of controlling the needed change in our lives to know when to retire, once we are able to.

And this change, this new life of retirement, needs a voice. A voice that may describe the change. A voice of hope, rather than the voice of anger and despair that often emerges with age and change. A voice that speaks to the spirit, the mind, and the body.

On the subject of the *spirit*, it begins to circle around to simpler times of childhood and again questions our most basic assumptions. As it looks back on a life of work and family and looks forward to a life of slowing down, it seeks a simplicity and a reasonableness that can fit a vast array of life experience.

Close your eyes. Picture in your mind's eye a "mature" person with "wisdom." What do you picture? Probably not a person who hides their age—rather one who embraces it gracefully. Probably not a person who is driven by a world of schedules, phone calls, meetings, interruptions, but rather a person who controls their world and does things because they want to and because they understand what kinds of things are good and important for them. Probably not a person driven to be kept busy with recreation or occupation, but rather a person who is not afraid to be alone with themselves and to pursue activities that are aligned with their personal spirit. Probably not an impatient person, but rather a person who recognizes that their opinion is just that—and not the one truth or fact—and patiently listens to others, providing their view when asked but not worrying if they are not asked or heard.

The spirit of retirement should feel wise. People are human and are always subject to impulse or distraction, but at a certain age they should also become wiser. Moving forward with grace may be more important to us than trying to retain all that should naturally slip from our hands—not in resignation, but in wisdom.

On the subject of the *mind*, it worries, and it has more time to think. It hears the clock ticking, the mainspring slowly winding down. The song must fill in the subject lines and calm the mind.

As we enter the final twenty-five- to thirty-year period of our lives, we should be able to reflect upon our lives and find joy and meaning. If not, then there is a lot more work to do and plenty of time to do it. Since we will be somewhat less active than in employed occupations and our "meaning" will be less defined by receiving paychecks, paying tuition bills, professional achievement, or daily family life, we will need to rely more and more on the spiritual and less and less on the "occupational" and "material" aspects of our days.

There is an art in the transition from acting to witnessing, from "producing" to reflecting, and not always continuing to "help" where "needed." The work involved in building a spiritual framework that is truly ours (not just given to us), that we understand and believe in, might be a source of great joy that many choose to default on and miss a great period of life.

On the subject of the *body*, it is changing and its role is changing. No longer required to have the stamina of work schedule, and with small but perceptible physical limitations becoming more apparent, the approach to exercise and recreation changes with the growing application of analgesics and painkillers. More than earlier phases of life, this is one of acceptance of limitations rather than striving for new capacity. The cellular time clock of the body runs on lithium batteries and quartz crystals that accurately and relentlessly mark the passage of time that we can limit only a little, if at all. Nothing is wrong with staying "in shape," exercising and eating well, as long as it does not become so pathological that it begins to numb our spiritual senses and blinds us to our reality, limiting our experiencing a truly great part of life. As the Grand Prix drivers will tell you, it is often necessary to "slow down to go fast," to think and follow the right line to be the fastest, to drive smart in order to win the race, rather than mindlessly trashing the car, as many new novice drivers do. As our bodies change, we must slow down too and think in order to proceed more quickly to find health and happiness rather than frustration.

One can argue that these divisions are artificial, or that this book is overly focused on the spirit . . . and that may be true. There is tremendous overlap in the themes of the poems. But the spirit is that human element that is often most neglected, that is most central to our survival, and that must be found and understood.

A plan is needed. Not a self-help book, but a map of the opportunities that retirement can be.

And most of all, we need a new tune to hum—a song that sets down a new beat and rhythm to life after retirement, that changes the march to light jazz with enough rock 'n' roll to stir the blood, and loses the blues and certainly the dirge, and trumpets the freedom of retirement.

My poems are unstructured and free verse . . . they do not rhyme. Retirement is certainly that way—free and lacking much of the structure and predictable rhythm of work-life, it may not fit a particular pattern. It is simpler, but it lacks the transparent simplicity of childhood . . . as our thoughts circle back to our earlier times and rhymes, but also remain conditioned and complicated by our life experience. I hope the style of the poetry makes them more accessible, if, perhaps, less artful.

The poems may appear to be overly dark and pessimistic, but that is a misimpression—they are not intended to be. They seek to face life and move forward by putting words and pictures to the complex passage of retirement. Facing down key parts of life, be it the importance of career, family, personal reputation and identity, the good (or bad) we do to others, the death of friends, or our view of our purpose, I hope they emerge as, at least, true, and, I hope, optimistic.

The poems may appear to be religious, but they are not. As my book, *The New Enlightenment*, and my many articles describe, I personally find my version of God, the spirit, and humanity in reason and reasonableness, but not in rules, ritual, and doctrine. For clarity on what I mean by "God" and "spirit," refer to my book and articles.

Some have questioned why I have written this section at all, to introduce and explain the poems. True poets are never supposed to explain themselves—the poems are supposed to stand on their own. Many would argue that it detracts from the poems. I have several answers to that. I have spent my career as a consultant and teacher—old habits die hard. I also take a note from Tom Wolfe's *The Painted Word*, in which he argues, partially tongue in cheek, that modern art often benefits so much from its

paragraphs of critical explanation that we might be bet-
ter served by mounting the explanation and throwing the
painting/sculpture away. And, finally, as I said earlier, I
want the ideas to be as accessible as possible, as a book of
philosophy masquerading as a collection of poetry. In any
case, I've reached that age when I generally feel compelled
to "explain what I mean," and I have.

So, I put my poems forward as the way I hear this
song—perhaps you will like some of them and begin to
hum along with me.

A DISCUSSION OF THE POETRY

Poems of the Spirit

One of the disorienting features (and a marker of further loss of identity and meaning) of retirement, for those who have worked all of their lives and felt in full control of their lives, is that it brings on a period of dependence where earning a living in a controlled way through work is replaced by worrying about the stability of pension plans, markets, and financial instruments, most of which are out of our immediate control.

It is more than a little unnerving to sense this relative lack of control, to wonder if we have planned well or if we could suffer huge and debilitating surprises from unexpected economic changes and market swings. It can certainly keep us awake at night to think about our *Fixed Income*.

"Fixed income" may also reference our spiritual capital that we have been investing in for decades. How will we use our memories and experiences, our little rewards and treasures that we have worked so hard to accumulate and save, our spiritual 401(k)s, as we enter this last phase of our lives?

And, of course, the genetics of our bodies dictate that we are living on physical "fixed income," our time of life that we can squander, hoard, or spend wisely.

Similarly, to pretend to be forever young, to cling to a younger image of ourselves as a denial of our aging, is in many ways to deny ourselves and is pointless and futile . . . and in many ways sad, both for the transparent masquerade and for the squandering of important experiences and passages. It also denies the value of the wisdom and experience that have been acquired over our lives.

On the outside, we may physically be able to do many of the same things we could do when we were younger, and we may be physically fit and healthy for many years. And it is a tribute to the human spirit that people try to keep themselves healthy and in good physical condition. On the other hand, our clock is ticking, and it is important to add a little more effort to the process of detaching our spiritual nature and perspective from the material world. To conclude our lives without additional deep reflection on our spiritual nature, especially in the later phases of our lives, is to both throw away a huge portion of the wisdom and knowledge that we have accumulated over the years and also deny ourselves the opportunity to build the grace and peace that comes with reflection on the spirit. Facelifts do not fully prepare you for eternity.

Inside, of course, we are all still young in many ways. We often see ourselves as we were when we were growing up and full of energy and vitality and fresh beauty. And it is central to our spirit to be able to connect to the earlier periods in our lives. But it is also important to recognize that physically we have changed and to enjoy that change with grace . . . or irony . . . or both.

I recall a recent scene at the beach when a young girl

called me "*Sir.*"

As we go through life, our many phases are defined by our age, our roles, our economic conditions. As people work to build themselves and their lives, their structures define them with schedules, responsibilities, and a variety of pressures to grow and succeed, which may range from meetings and work products to carpools and dinner planning to soccer games and summer vacation plans.

And much of that tends to change at retirement. There is no need to set the alarm clock. The meetings at work do not beckon, the carpools are over, the kids are on their own and call periodically . . . the schedules, if there are any, are much simpler and less demanding.

It is easy to begin to think that we are just disappearing. It is easy to begin to think that we just no longer matter. As I sit on a Northern California beach and watch the fog come in, I can begin to feel *Fogged In*.

We may still feel young, but one of the facts of retirement age is that people we know start dying off at a faster rate.

The most dramatic sign to me of "creeping disappearance" and "fog" is the death of the friends or key players in my life that I tend to call my "life witnesses." These have been the people that I have set up as milestones and benchmarks for my life. They may be parents or siblings, rivals, bosses, teachers, friends, or others who know where I started and saw what I did from various perspectives that are important to me. They are people who may have seen me do something that I regarded as important, or they may be people whom I wanted to impress for one reason or another. They may represent failures that I worked hard to overcome. They are unique to my life and my way of viewing it. Many of them would have no idea that I conferred any importance on them at all. So much of our "real" life takes place only in our own heads. But they were important to me, and as they pass from the scene, a chunk of my life and its secret scorekeeping passes away forever. As they disappear, it is almost as if the family albums have been burned up in a fire, along with those *Witnesses*.

As with all the important parts of our lives, our connections are always bittersweet, if only because they come and go. But, as with most things, the answer is in the human spirit. The point is that our life's witnesses were important touchstones that helped define us, create meaning, and, through those many odd connections, helped us better understand the ways in which all of us are connected to one another.

I think it takes some time and perspective to look back and fully appreciate central parts of our life experiences, such as our "witnesses." Our real life is our thoughts and memories, and retirement provides a useful milepost for reflection and appreciation of the patterns and connections that life affords each of us. And it is never too late to create a new life.

So, at retirement or turning sixty, get out those old photo albums and remember the times of life long forgotten. Maybe make a list of your "life's witnesses." The list itself, the people who were important to you, may tell you a lot about your life and who you really are. Do an accounting, take stock, but then move on.

Beyond our witnesses, we have our skills, our beliefs, our reputations, our money, our families, our occupations—will they have the importance and meaning that we thought they would have as we built and saved them all these many years? Were they worth it? Can we live on them for future years? Do we have enough to draw on to support us spiritually in the last third of our lives? Will we become bored and aimless, or will we have an endless (or at least sufficient) supply of energy? Or should we do a serious housecleaning in our retirement, and free ourselves to fully enjoy this new phase of our life, through better distinguishing between our *Windows and Mirrors*?

Many of these thoughts come together with the iconic passage of our sixtieth birthday—that decade milestone in all lives—often the scene of the great going-away parties, or at least the beginning of that season.

When we realize that the number of days ahead is so likely less than the number of days behind, and a growing list of friends and acquaintances find their end of days, it tends to alter the restless thoughts of 4:30 a.m. from family and job to death and our many gambles on an afterlife. That's why it's called *The Big "6-O."*

For the vast majority, retirement presents a huge life passage that creates an anxious scramble for new perspective and some closure. Self-definition and meaning can no longer come from work—be it employment or raising a family. Certainty on long-held faiths and truths often suddenly fades as we go to sleep or wake up contemplating death. What seemed so important and right when we were younger may not be the same as what has slowly become the center of our lives. We lose our bearing and wonder what we've made of ourselves.

Steve Jobs once delivered a great commencement address in which he said that we can never really plan or anticipate or understand our lives looking forward (Man plans/God laughs). We have to connect the dots looking backward and try to figure out, if we can, what it all means. It may be very different from what we expected. And the reconnecting may turn out to be wonderful. And we may get a lot of surprises and a little amusement. As we mature, we discover that our lives were never what we anticipated because life comes without an operating manual. And you invent it, but you cannot control it all. But you can always tinker because there was *Some Assembly Required*.

Our bodies are not timeless, but our spirits may well be. The problem is that the material culture that surrounds us does not fully acknowledge this passage nor provide much spiritual guidance for our reinvention.

We may conclude that our *real* version of the spirit and of God is very different than the versions we adopted through religion or our culture. We have reached that last chance in our lives to put aside ideas given to us by others and to articulate to ourselves what we really think. We have only one life and it goes by quickly enough, and so we should build a reasonable framework that makes sense to us and that we can comfortably adopt. We must own it.

What a luxury, to have a time in our lives for consolidation and reflection. Those who accept spiritual frameworks from others, based upon "scriptures" or traditions, may be permanently handicapping themselves because they may be making their own spirits mute in the process—the spirit is to guide us, but if we shut the door to guidance, we may be turning on the spirit. One of the real tests of our lives, of whether we have really learned anything useful in life, is whether we can conclude our lives with a full and open reflection of what we've seen and observed, and whether our beliefs really reflect our spiritual nature, combined with rational reflection, driven through the lens of what is really reasonable to us to believe. That is the magic of living, perhaps best expressed in a set of *Haikus*.

And our spirits are sorely tested at retirement. For most, it represents an important passage, a mark in time. It confirms that we are getting older (why else would people "retire," i.e., "withdraw," "quit"?), and so most can hear the bell tolling and they know it tolls for them. As doctors move into overdrive with tests, warnings, and prescriptions, and as we see those birthdays tick off, our darkest thoughts turn to our mortality and death. And it is at that point that our faiths are put to their greatest test. Can we continue still to believe in the impossible anthropomorphic God, or in the urban-baroque, celestial Heaven? Can we believe that the rules and scorecards of our preferred religion represent the true alchemy to gain us "salvation" and eternal life (while billions of others choose the wrong religion and fail)? Can we believe in the improbable uniqueness of humanity as a truly timeless, spiritual creature? Or do we apply rationality, and even worse, reasonableness, and begin to falter, doubt, and perhaps even to despair? Do we begin the steep decline into depression as we resolutely march to oblivion? Any thoughtful and sensitive human would face these dilemmas and might come away with great unease.

Or . . . has the wisdom of our many years allowed us to observe that shadow of our lives that suggests the spirit in the many miracles that occur each day? Can we begin to search inward and find that spiritual motivation that confirms God and our souls and gains us confidence, and even joy, in our humanity and our timeless spirit that may not fully pass the test of rational, but is more than reasonable? Can we at least resolve our anxieties in the realm of the agnostic? We are truly tested to find the right path as we get older and "retire," and we have time and a certain imperative to think more intensely about what we truly believe. There comes a time to chose between hope and despair. At that point, the magnetic attraction of optimism is a truly unique human trait as we find our way among *The Black Path or the White Path*.

Poems of the Mind

Retirement—palace or jail cell; we actually get to choose. We need to develop the right perspective and have the right attitude, or we may find ourselves doing *Hard Time in the Big House*.

People really fear boredom, perhaps more than most other fates. What will I do if I'm not always occupied? We find many retirees at the golf course, looking for someone to play a round with; others, torn loose from their moorings, spend more time at the gym . . . or the bar. Still others may throw themselves into hobbies, new businesses, or even community service. Some may just watch TV. None of that is bad, but it does raise a question of "companionship strategy," once the regimented companionship of the workplace and raising a family is removed. People find many ways to address this issue through social media. Don't tell anyone—it's sad—but one of my favorites is *Midnight Online Poker*.

All of which leads me to the one great trap of most of our lives. We allow our occupations to replace us. We become what we do, which sells our souls to the lowest bidder and makes us an empty shell when it is all taken away at retirement. We do not know ourselves and do not enjoy our own company. Of course, we have to work and produce and support other people—that does give meaning to our lives—as long as it doesn't become us and leave us few, if any, other real ways to nourish our soul. I submit the following prayer on *Occupational Hazards*.

A good deal of our attitude at retirement may be caused by a lack of balance and confidence. We have entered a new phase and are having trouble adjusting. It is easy to say that it should all be taken with grace, but we have a sense of loss, a sense that a lot has been taken away from us—our roles, our dignity, our value. And this is all very frustrating and confusing to us, because we want people to need us, and we want to use some of the fantastic variety of skills, information, and wisdom that we have accumulated over many years, which now seems to have become oddly undervalued. Quite simply, at retirement, we find ourselves *Overqualified.*

A very tough realization in life is that most of the ideas, information, and experiences that we (and billions of others) accumulated in life will never be used by anybody. The whole world is a massive, inefficient system of redundancy. God's plan seems really sloppy and wasteful. We can try to teach and tell stories, but younger people prize brevity in older people and prefer to only hear the story a finite number of times. Youth must learn for itself in order to really learn. We need to come to the realization comfortably that acquiring our knowledge should have been a pleasure and privilege to us, and it is not squandered or wasted if we cannot convey it all to others. We can and should try to convey that which we think is useful, we should do it in small doses and at appropriate times, and we should not get frustrated if it does not all get through. The world has many paths to teach wisdom, and we are each but a small part of that process.

That is our humanity, and it should give us all great comfort. We do not need to do it all.

One of the hallmarks of getting older is how your attitude tends to amplify your thoughts and emotions. It shows up especially in how you see yourself, but more importantly, how you see others seeing you and how you act toward them. "Grumpy old man" is often more than a figure of speech. As we cycle back to simpler ideas and behavior, often somewhat childlike, seasoned with . . . well, seasons . . . and hopefully worldly wisdom, we sometimes become less guarded and more unrestrained in voicing our views—what I might call "Retirement Tourette's."

Our little quirks, which might have been somewhat charming or at least acceptable in earlier ages, become magnified into what are often very annoying habits. We may become a little annoyed . . . we may become more paranoid, or at least what others might term, with not a little patronization, "too sensitive." There are definite psychological changes to reflect on. After sixty-plus years, we feel somewhat entitled to voice our views—others may not be quite as ready to listen to them. And, so, we should never get *too* sensitive. We should trust in ourselves and in others. We may just need a better *Hearing Aid.*

When we reach a certain age, we get the largely incorrect idea that life will be easier. We think we have paid our dues over the years and should be given a little latitude—a little respect. It is certainly an expectation that we have for our kids. While many of us are blessed with wonderful children, we often have the feeling that we're not given the deference due. It is a hollow expectation and one that we should grow out of. It is an expectation that minimizes us and suggests a more limited range of understanding of others, belying our age and would-be wisdom. We need to dispense with pretension and see family and children through a variety of lenses, the most powerful of which should be love. Younger people can become strange and annoying, or they can be seen as the wonderful, exciting, but different (sort of) creatures that they are. They are always our *Little Angels/Lying Dogs.*

As we reflect on the patterns in life, it should cause us to recognize our own role for others and to be good (and conscious) witnesses for them, just as many have served as witnesses for us. Sometimes, especially as we get older, our "passive role" is our most important contribution—little comments of support, helpful hints of wisdom, just being there to provide confirmation—and can have more impact that the more active things we "do."

Can you measure the value when you are more a witness than a participant . . . more an audience than a player?

Of course. The participants and players have little real value without the witnesses and audience. It is so important to be there to witness, to encourage, to share what wisdom has been gained over many years (without "overvaluing" the wisdom as it is shared), to provide coaching and guidance without trying to push the young players off the stage—it is their stage, and we are in the audience now . . . and audience participation is highly discouraged.

If we're wise, we should just settle down and enjoy our *Orchestra Seats*.

Often, our views of the world and ourselves are re-flected in our views of others, especially our spouses. As we get older, we may make the mistake of taking the scorecard out too often, and perhaps we may even change the measures—but that may not reflect how others see themselves or us at all. And so, it is especially important to see if we can see ourselves in others and understand how they may see themselves in us. That may tell us a lot about what we have become—which may well allow us to approach each new reunion less as a drudgery, but more as an opportunity. I remember well *My Wife's Fortieth High School Reunion*.

A very similar point can be made about spouses and the complex institution that is a strong and sustained marriage. Somehow we expect that relationships will simply get easier and smoother the older we get and the longer we are together. Can you hear the train wreck coming along with that idea? It suggests a real misconception about what a great relationship really is and how we should mature with our closest friend. Great and sustained relationships are an *Acquired Taste*.

Poems of the Body

One of life's inevitabilities is that our bodies change and slow down a little when we get older or retire. For today's hardworking type A generation, this creates some interesting problems, as people who have lived on adrenaline since their college days, and some from high school and grammar school, actually need to slow down a little to stay healthy. People who attacked life and were sensitive to each tick of the clock—the "multitaskers," the "time optimizers," and the "one-minute (usually a New York minute) managers"—need to slow down and stop training for their version of the Life Olympics. It is a spiritual adjustment as much as a physical adjustment—it is a different understanding of goals and methods. It is time for the *Adrenaline Junky/Cold Turkey*.

No reflection on retirement and the body would be complete without golf. Whether you play the game or not, you are stuck with the enduring image of the retiree on the golf course . . . or hundreds of golf courses . . . of all kinds . . . everywhere. And, of course, golf gives us some great metaphors for life.

You start out with huge energy and expectation by hitting the ball hard and have it launch off into the sky with a multitude of unexpected opportunities . . . or hazards. You can literally join the ball in its flight. You face many unexpected situations and hazards along the way. As you proceed down the fairway, you need to be more careful and more precise to get a good score. Finally, you need to really slow down with your putting and end with a great deal of precision. And, of course, the end is a hole in the ground.

Similarly, the Buddhists have a lot to offer here . . . golf is a Zen game. You need to swing slower to get the ball to go further. You hit down on the ball to get it to go up. You should often play the shorter club to get the ball to the green and in the hole with fewer strokes. There is a certain restraint and required patience in golf that suggests a wisdom we wished we had and could teach.

And, for retirement, there is a lot we can learn from tackling the *15th Hole*.

The other great retirement game is, of course, "symptoms." In our conversational sleight of hand, we replace "What do you do?" with "How do you feel?" There is a special place in hell for all of those who lead off by telling me "You look good" or "You've got great color." What would retirement be without worrying about cancer, colonoscopies, statins, and Metamucil . . . symptoms and treatments . . . the baseball trading cards of old age. We are physical creatures, and our systems do turn on us from time to time. As the hyperactive type A that we are, we turn our attention to aches, pains, and recent medical alerts. Everyone seems to have read all of the latest studies from the *New England Journal of Medicine*. Although the life expectancy in the U.S. is very high, everyone looks for the telltale signs in *The Garden*.

At a certain age, it all comes down to this: do you have a pulse? Literally and figuratively? Spiritually, mentally, and physically? At retirement, the music changes. Certainly a little grace is in order, and a nocturne is most welcome. A little spice is also needed, and some light jazz background music really seems so often just right. A march is a little more than I'd like to deal with. But if I could sum it up, I'm still looking for a little hard rap, a fun, exuberant, primal scream at oblivion. A scream that says, "Here I am," "This is what I am," and "This is how I got here."

So, how to sum it up? To square the circle of religion, science, and our lives, and what we can conclude from a lifetime that makes sense to us. To decide if we evolved from the material or were selected and designed by the divine . . . or if that debate really matters at all. To figure out, as we age, where we're headed. As we grow older and, hopefully, evolve, do we side with all we've heard from physics and biology, or from the Bible and Koran, or all, or none? Do we see the pattern in things? Do we understand life and change? In the end, we might decide it's time for a road trip to find some answers in the *Galapagos*.

And so, it's not about the past and what we've done or lost, and it's not about the future and what might or might not happen—it has always been, and is only, about now. Live life, for real, and do not fear anything.

—Grady

ABOUT THE AUTHOR

Grady Means is retired, having spent his life working in government and managing businesses, as well as writing and speaking about business and management, politics, foreign affairs, and religion.

Grady served in government as Assistant to Vice President Rockefeller in the White House and as an economist working on health, poverty, and human welfare issues at the U.S. Department of Health, Education, and Welfare.

He practiced management consulting for thirty years and was a managing partner at PriceWaterhouseCoopers, running billion-dollar businesses focused on corporate strategy consulting and government consulting.

He has written best-selling books on business and economics, as well as a more recent book on religion and politics. He has authored many newspaper and magazine articles on business, politics, and religion.

At this stage of his life, he launches and manages startup businesses, writes, rides his motorcycle, hikes, sails, surfs, golfs, spends time with family, but, for the most part, just thinks about things.

He splits his time between the East and West Coasts.